Easy Classic Recorder Duets

With one very easy part, and the other more difficult. Favourite melodies from the world's greatest composers arranged especially for two recorders, starting with the easiest. All in easy keys.

Amanda Oosthuizen
Jemima Oosthuizen

The Ruby Recorder series
Wild Music Publications

We hope you enjoy *Easy Classic Recorder Duets!*

Take a look at other exciting books in the series
Including: *Christmas Duets, Trick or Treat – A Halloween Suite, More Christmas Duets, Classic Duets for Intermediate players, 50+ Greatest Classics, Easy Traditional Duets, Easy Tunes from Around the World,* and many more!

For more information on other amazing books please go to:
http://WildMusicPublications.com

For a **free** sample of our book of **Christmas Carols** (no need to download if you already have the book!) AND a **free play-along backing track** visit:

http://WildMusicPublications.com/**secret3-recorder4-tracks5/**

And use the password: **RazzleDazzleRecorder**

Happy Music Making!

The Wild Music Publications Team

To keep up –to-date with our new releases, why not
follow us on Twitter

@WMPublications

© Copyright 2016 Wild Music Publications

The music in this book is protected by copyright and may not be reproduced in any way for sale or private use without the consent of the author.

Contents

Allegretto - Diabelli 30

Allegro, Eine Kleine Nachtmusik - Mozart 7

Allegro - Haydn 16

Brindisi, La Traviata – Verdi 26

Carrillon - Bizet 24

Dance of the Hours, La Gioconda – Ponchielli 12

Finale, Carnival of the Animals – Saint Saëns 31

Galop and Can-Can, Orpheus in the Underworld – Offenbach 23

Gavotte - Gossec 6

Grand Waltz, Opus 18 – Chopin 10

La Bamba - Traditional 14

La Cucuracha - Traditional 20

La Paloma - Yradier 42

Lullaby - Brahms 5

March, Nutcracker Suite – Tchaikovsky 17

Mazurka, Coppelia – Delibes 19

Musette - Gluck 10

Pizzicato Polka – J.Strauss 9

Plaisir d'Amour - Martini 11

Queen of the Night Aria, The Magic Flute - Mozart 38

Radetsky March – J.Strauss 13

Russian Dance - Tchaikovsky 44

Spring, The Four Seasons – Vivaldi 2

The Sorcerer's Apprentice – Dukas 26

Toreador's Song, Carmen – Bizet 4

Voi Che Sapete, Marriage of Figaro – Mozart 3

Waltz – Delibes 2

Spring
from *The Four Seasons*

Antonio Vivaldi
(1678-1741)

Bright and Cheerful

Voi Che Sapete
from *The Marriage of Figaro*

Wolfgang Amadeus Mozart
(1756-1791)

Toreador's Song
from *Carmen*

Georges Bizet
(1838-1875)

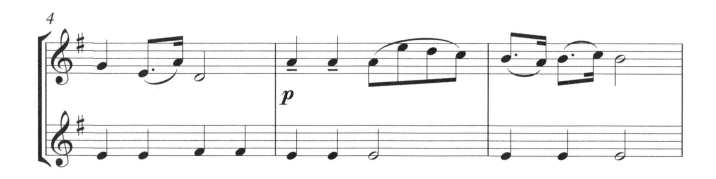
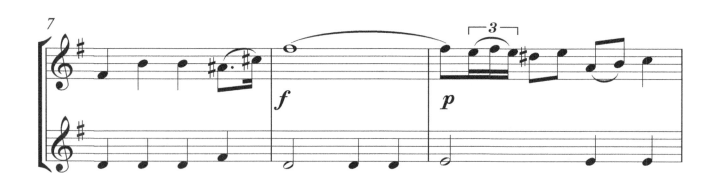
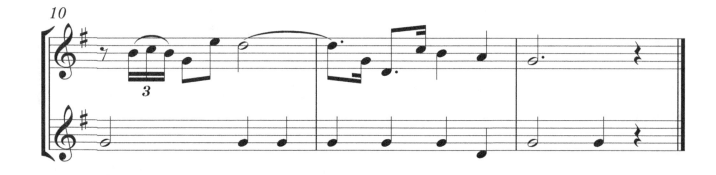

Lullaby

Johannes Brahms
(1833-1897)

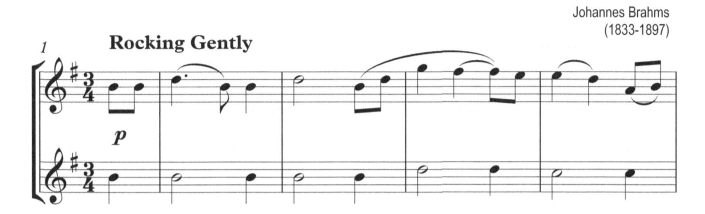

Gavotte

Francois-Joseph Gossec
(1734-1829)

Allegro
from *Eine Kleine Nachtmusik*

Wolfgang Amadeus Mozart
(1756-1791)

Dance of the Hours
from *La Gioconda*

Amilcare Ponchielli
(1834-1886)

Pizzicato Polka

Johann Strauss
(1825-1899)

Musette

Christoph Willibald Gluck
(1714-1787)

Plaisir d'Amour

Jean-Paul-Égide Martini
(1741-1816)

Grand Waltz
Opus 18

Frédéric Chopin
(1810-1849)

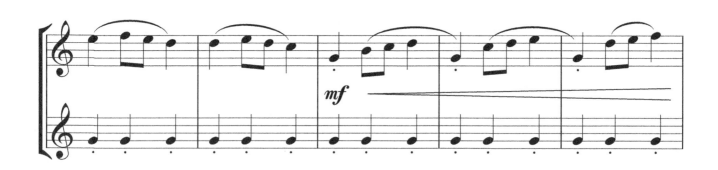
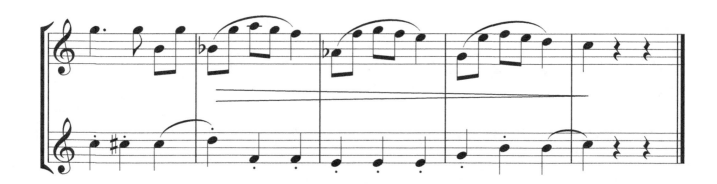

Radetzky March

Johann Strauss
(1825-1899)

La Bamba

Spain

Allegro

Franz Joseph Haydn
(1732-1809)

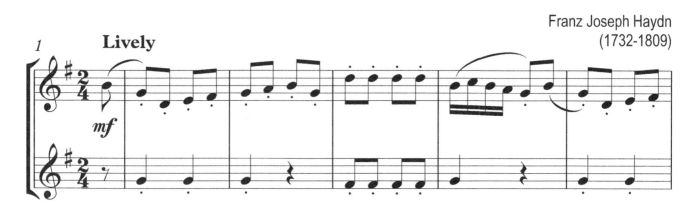

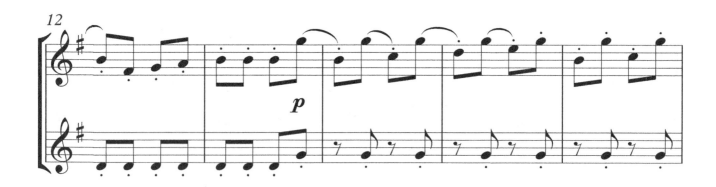

March
from *The Nutcracker Suite*

Pyotr Ilyich Tchaikovsky
(1840-1893)

La Cucuracha

Mexico

Mazurka

Leo Delibes
(1836-1891)

Carillon

Georges Bizet
(1838-1875)

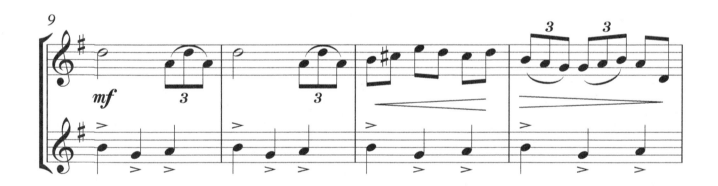

The Sorcerer's Apprentice

Paul Dukas
(1865-1935)

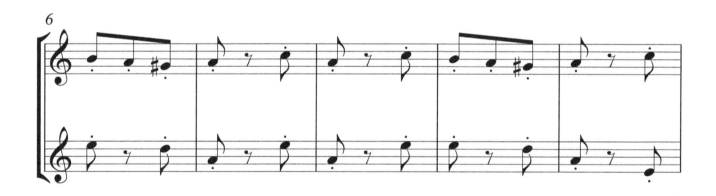

27

Waltz

Leo Delibes
(1836-1891)

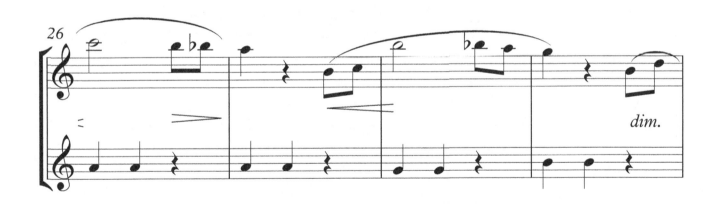

Allegretto

Anton Diabelli
(1751-1858)

31

Galop and Can-Can
from *Orpheus in the Underworld*

Jacques Offenbach
(1819-1880)

Finale
from *Carnival of the Animals*

Camille Saint-Saëns
(1835-1921)

35

Brindisi

from *La Traviata*

Giuseppe Verdi
(1813-1901)

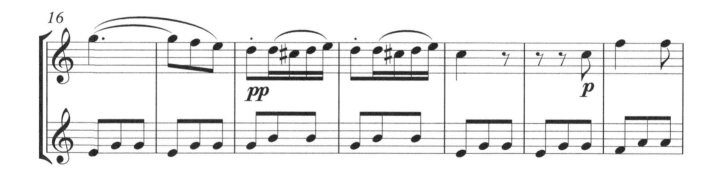

The Queen of the Night Aria

from *The Magic Flute*

Wolfgang Amadeus Mozart
(1756-1791)

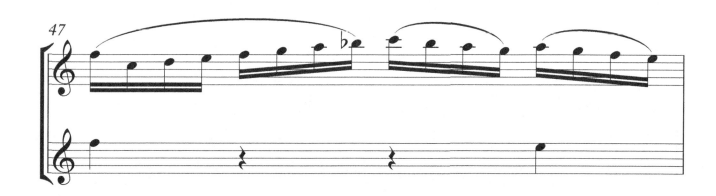

La Paloma

Sebastian Yradier
(1809-1865)

Russian Dance

from *The Nutcracker*

Pyotr Ilyich Tchaikovsky
(1840-1893)

Information

Tempo Markings

Adagio – slow and stately
Adagio lamentoso – slowly and sadly
Alla Marcia – like a march
Allegretto – moderately fast
Allegretto pomposo – fast and pompous
Allegro – fast and bright
Allegro assai – very fast
Allegro grazioso – fast and gracefully
Allegro maestoso – fast and majestically
Allegro vivace – fast and lively
Andante – at walking speed
Andante maestoso – a majestic walk
Andante moderato – a moderately fast
Andante non troppo – Not too fast
Andantino – slightly faster (or sometimes slower) than Andante
Andantino ingueno – not fast but with innocence
Lento - slowly
Maestoso - majestically
Moderato - moderately
Moderato con moto – moderately with movement
Molto allegro – very fast
Molto maestoso – very majestically
Presto – extremely fast
Tempo di mazurka – In the time of a mazurka - lively
Tempo di valse – In the time of a waltz
Vivace – lively and fast
Vivo - lively

Tempo Changes

rall. – rallentando – gradually slowing down
rit. – ritenuto – slightly slower

 fermata – pause on this note

Dynamic Markings

dim. – diminuendo – gradually softer
cresc. – crescendo – gradually louder
cresc. poco a poco al fine – gradually louder towards the end

pp – *pianissiomo* – very softly
p – *piano* – softly
mp – *mezzo piano* – moderately soft
mf – *mezzo forte* – moderately loud
f – *forte* – loud
ff – *fortissimo* – very loud

gradually louder
gradually softer

Repeats

D.C. al Coda – return to the beginning and follow signs to Coda ⊕
D.C. al Fine – return to the beginning and play to *Fine*

A repeated passage is to be played with a different ending.

Articulation

staccato – short and detached
sempre staccato – play staccato throughout

accent – played with attack

tenuto – held– pressured accent

marcato – forcefully

Ornaments

trill – rapid movement to the note above and back or from the note above in Mozart and earlier music.

mordent – three rapid notes – the principal note, the note above and the principal.

acciaccatura – a very quick note

appoggiatura – divide the main note equally between the two notes.

If you have enjoyed **Easy Classic Recorder Duets,** why not try the other books in the **Ruby Recorder** series!

For more info, please visit: **WildMusicPublications.com**

All of our books are available to download, or you can order from Amazon.

Introducing some of our favourites:

Champagne and Chocolate

50+ Greatest Classics

Christmas Carols

Trick or Treat – A Halloween Suite

Easy Traditional Duets

Easy Tunes from Around the World

Classic Duets for Intermediate Players

Christmas Duets

Moonlight and Roses

Made in the USA
Las Vegas, NV
18 March 2024

87385773R00031